W9-ABX-823

FIRST
PEOPLES
of NORTH
AMERICA

THE PEOPLE AND
CULTURE OF THE
CROW

RAYMOND BIAL

Cavendish
Square

New York

Published in 2016 by Cavendish Square Publishing, LLC
243 5th Avenue, Suite 136, New York, NY 10016

Website: cavendishsq.com

This publication represents the opinions and views of the author based on his or her personal experience, knowledge, and research. The information in this book serves as a general guide only. The author and publisher have used their best efforts in preparing this book and disclaim liability rising directly or indirectly from the use and application of this book.

CPSIA Compliance Information: Batch #CW16CSQ

All websites were available and accurate when this book was sent to press.

Library of Congress Cataloging-in-Publication Data

Bial, Raymond.
The people and culture of the Crow / Raymond Bial.
pages cm. — (First peoples of North America)
Includes bibliographical references and index.
ISBN 978-1-5026-1000-3 (hardcover) ISBN 978-1-5026-1001-0 (ebook)
1. Crow Indians—History—Juvenile literature.
2. Crow Indians—Social life and customs—Juvenile literature. I. Title.
E99.C92B53 2016
978.6004'975272—dc23

2015023312

Editorial Director: David McNamara
Editor: Kristen Susienka
Copy Editor: Nathan Heidelberger
Art Director: Jeffrey Talbot
Designer: Amy Greenan
Senior Production Manager: Jennifer Ryder-Talbot
Production Editor: Renni Johnson
Photo Research: J8 Media

The photographs in this book are used by permission and through the courtesy of: Public Domain/Fred E. Miller-Spotted Rabbit (Crow tribe) on horseback, Montana.jpg/Wikimedia Commons, cover; ullstein bild/Getty Images, backcover; Raymond Bial, 6, 18, 22, 24, 27, 29, 33, 37, 38, 44, 59, 91; Steve Bower/Shutterstock.com, 8; Public Domain/British Library/Old time Peegan squaw with travois and papoose (HS85-10-18748).jpg/Wikimedia Commons, 11; Peter Newark American Pictures/Bridgeman Images, 19; Library of Congress, 20, 31, 40, 42, 46, 68, 69, 76, 78, 80, 104, 106, 107, 108; Don Schuhart, USDA Natural Resources Conservation Service/NRCSMT90001 - Montana (5049)(NRCS Photo Gallery).jpg/Wikimedia Commons, 43; Murphy_Shewchuk/iStockphoto.com, 50; Djembayz/Crow beaded moccasins from around 1940.JPG/Wikimedia Commons, 55; Public Domain/Smithsonian American Art Museum/Hó-ra-tó-a, a Brave.jpg/Wikimedia Commons, 57; Annie Griffiths Belt/Getty Images, 62; Jeffrey B. Banke/Shutterstock.com, 64; Werner Forman Archive/Bridgeman Images, 66; Bobbi Onia/Underwood Archives/Getty Images, 71; Heeb Christian/Age Fotostock, 72–73; UniversalImagesGroup/Getty Images, 80; Ted Thai/The LIFE Images Collection/Getty Images, 82; Curtis Martin/Getty Images, 85; John Rous/AP Images, 93; Kmusser/CrowIRmap.png/Wikimedia Commons, 94; Lawrence Migdale/Getty Images, 96; Allen Russell/Alamy, 97; AF archive/Alamy, 99; Matthew Brown/AP Images, 101; Look and Learn/Bridgeman Images, 103.

Printed in the United States of America

ACKNOWLEDGMENTS

This book would not have been possible without the help
of many organizations and individuals, including several
who have devoted themselves to preserving the traditions
and improving the life of the Crow people in Montana.
I am indebted to everyone on the Crow reservation at
Crow Agency, Montana, for permission to make photographs
there. I especially enjoyed visiting Crow Fair, which is the
largest annual gathering of Native people in North America.

I would like to thank everyone at Cavendish Square
Publishing for their input on *The People and Culture of
the Crow* and the other books in the First Peoples of North
America series. As always, I offer my deepest appreciation
to my wife, Linda, and my children Anna, Sarah, and Luke
for their wonderful inspiration.

CONTENTS

Many Crow children learn to ride horses at a young age.

AUTHOR'S NOTE

At the dawn of the twentieth century, Native Americans were thought to be a vanishing race. However, despite four hundred years of warfare, deprivation, and disease, Native Americans have persevered. Countless thousands have lost their lives, but over the course of this century and the last, the populations of Native tribes have grown tremendously. Even as America's First People struggle to adapt to modern Western life, they have also kept the flame of their traditions alive—the languages, religions, stories, and the everyday ways of life. An exhilarating renaissance in Native American culture is now sweeping the continent from coast to coast.

The First Peoples of North America books depict the social and cultural life of the major nations, from the early history of Native peoples in North America to their present-day struggles for survival and dignity. Historical and contemporary photographs of traditional subjects, as well as period illustrations, are blended throughout each book so that readers may gain a sense of family life in a tipi, a hogan, or a longhouse.

No single book can comprehensively portray the intricate and varied lifeways of an entire tribe, or nation. I only hope that young people will come away with a deeper appreciation for the rich tapestry of Native American culture—both then and now—and a keen desire to learn more about these first Americans.

The Montana landscape is vast and mountainous.

CHAPTER ONE

There is no country like the Crow Country.

—Chief Arapoosh

A CULTURE BEGINS

For generations, the Crow Nation has called Montana its home. The Crow people have created communities under the state's rolling hills and blue skies. There, they have shaped their history, from the earliest times when the Crow's ancestors arrived in North America to the present day. Throughout the years, the Crow have formed traditions and maintained religious practices. Elders retell the stories of their ancestors from long ago. Their story has not been easy, however. Although they have persevered as a nation, they and their ancestors have endured hardships and difficulty. Still, today the Crow remain a respected and unique Native community, proud of their rich and varied heritage.

The Crow in North America

Like other Native peoples of North America, the ancestors of the Crow came from Siberia, most likely migrating across the **Bering Strait** over a narrow land bridge that once joined Asia and Alaska. According to Crow stories, the tribe lived in a land of many lakes, which was most likely around Lake Winnipeg in what is now the province of Manitoba, Canada. Over time, they moved southward and settled as a farming people in what are now the Dakotas, where they live today. These people are known as the Hidatsa. In the early 1600s, a powerful leader named No Vitals had a vision that instructed him to lead some of the Hidatsa west into the Rocky Mountains in search of a sacred tobacco plant. He thought that the tobacco seeds would give his people an identity as a tribe and keep them safe.

Therefore, sometime between the mid-1600s and early 1700s, about five hundred **band** members left the Hidatsa and moved to the plains of what are now southern Montana and northern Wyoming. Eventually they would be known as the Crow. These early Crow likely came from two groups: the Awatixa Hidatsa, who were the ancestors of the Mountain Crow, and the main Hidatsa, who are believed to be the ancestors of the River Crow. According to traditional stories, however,

Many Native Americans, including the Crow, traveled with sleds called travois (pictured here).

the Crow began as a single group that split into the Mountain and River divisions early in their history after an argument between two powerful chiefs. Long Hair led the Mountain Crow into the high country south of the Yellowstone River, while Arapoosh and the River Crow stayed north of the Yellowstone, along the Musselshell and Judith Rivers, which flow into the Missouri River.

A Siouan-speaking people, the Crow referred to themselves as **Absaroka** or Apsaalooke, which means "Children of the Long-Beaked Bird." Other Native peoples called them "Sparrowhawk," "Bird People," or "Crows," as they are now known. The Crow became **nomadic** hunters of the plentiful game, especially the large herds of buffalo that roamed the grasslands of their territory in present-day Montana. For hundreds of years they followed the herds in the northern **Great Plains**. The buffalo supplied nearly all their needs for food, clothing, and shelter. When game became scarce, they moved to another camp, relying on dogs to pull A-shaped **travois** (trav-OYZ), small sled-like carriers on which they loaded their belongings. The dogs also carried packs strapped on their backs.

Before the Spanish brought horses to North America in the 1600s, the Crow's way of life was very difficult. They were limited in their travel to the small loads a dog or person could carry on their backs or travois. However, they acquired horses around 1730, possibly from the Eastern Shoshone tribe, who became a major supplier of horses to the Crow and many other Plains Peoples. Thereafter, their way of life changed dramatically. Now that they could transport greater weights, the Crow made larger **tipis** (TEE-peez), at least double in size, and traveled farther from one camp to another. As the Crow learned to ride horses, they could race after the herds of buffalo, better defend themselves against their enemies, and trade with friendly tribes over broad stretches of prairie. Horses became so important to the tribe that a man's wealth was measured by the number of horses he owned. By the early 1800s, the Crow had more horses than any other tribe east of the Rockies—between twenty and sixty horses per household.

For nearly two centuries, the Crow moved from camp to camp, traveling over the waves of prairie grass that swept into the distance. Occasionally, the plains were broken by a stream lined with ragged trees. Much of the landscape was also rippled with low hills and ridges, along with a few isolated mountains, or buttes, rising abruptly from the rolling land. To the west, far into the distance, were the often white-capped Rocky Mountains.

This vast, open country, with the sky looming overhead, gave the Crow a great sense of freedom. The Mountain Crow hunted along broad, shallow rivers, notably the Bighorn, middle Yellowstone, upper Tongue, and Powder Rivers. They also pursued game up in the Bighorn, Absaroka, Beartooth, and Wind River Mountains. The River Crow ranged along the lower Yellowstone and north along the Marias and Milk Rivers, then turned into the Judith Basin for hunting in the fall and winter. The banks of these streams were fringed with cottonwood trees, whose leaves turned vivid yellow in the autumn. The Crow often camped near these rivers where the clear waters flowed through the grasslands. The stands of trees also gave them a degree of shelter from enemies and the weather, especially the wind and snow.

The Crow lived in a region of intense weather. Summers were hot, often with little rain, and winters tended to be brutally cold. Strong winds from the west and arctic north often brought heavy snows. One could be blinded by the swirling whiteness, get lost, and soon freeze to death. Yet the northern plains also had mild weather through the first green of spring, the bloom of summer, and the golden foliage of autumn. During warm weather, the plains were fragrant with the scent of sage, which covered much of the land. However, during these brief seasons, the Crow had to devote themselves to hunting and gathering in preparation for the next winter.

Many animals inhabited the plains of Crow territory. Huge herds of buffalo grazed the plains. Beneath the sea of grass there were prairie dog towns from which rodents popped up occasionally, only to plunge back into their burrows. Swift, graceful pronghorn antelope and wild horses raced across the plains. Birds tended carefully hidden nests on the ground, as hungry coyotes hunted for mice in clumps of grass. Overhead, vultures circled, while hawks and eagles soared in the updrafts. These birds of prey swooped down upon rabbits, mourning doves, and other small animals, while sandhill cranes waded through the shallow water along the edges of streams.

The rivers were home to many kinds of fish, including sturgeon and yellow bullhead. From mid-May through June, ancient paddlefish swam in the waters of the Yellowstone River, while trout zipped through the nearby Bighorn River. Up in the hills, elk, moose, bighorn sheep, and mule deer nibbled tufts of grass, while they remained alert for bobcats, mountain lions, wolves, black bears, and grizzlies. Wild turkeys, partridges, and grouse also foraged among the trees.

To the Crow, these plants and animals provided food, clothing, and shelter. But they were also sacred, as was the land itself.

A Culture of Stories

One of the oldest traditions of the Crow people is storytelling. For many years, the Crow had no way of writing down their language, stories, or history. They passed everything down through word of mouth, or oral tradition. Here is one story about the sun, who was known as **Old Man Coyote**, and how the earth and people came to be.

Long ago, there was no earth, only water, and the sole creatures were some ducks. Old Man Coyote came down to visit the ducks.

"My brothers," he said. "There is earth below us. It is not good for us to be alone."

He turned to a large mallard duck and suggested, "Dive down into the water and gather some earth. We will use it to make a place to live."

The mallard did as he was asked. He remained below for a long time, but came back without any soil.

Old Man Coyote then said to the pinto duck, "I sent an older one, but he did not get any earth. Now I will let you try."

The pinto duck dove into the deep. He was gone for a very long time, but also came up without earth.

"How is that?" Old Man Coyote asked. "I surely thought you would bring some soil back."

Turning to a small blue duck, Old Man Coyote said, "You must dive down into the water. If you do not bring up any soil, we will have no land to live on."

The blue-feathered duck did as he was asked, but he could not get any soil.

Old Man Coyote exclaimed, "If you are such poor divers, we will never have any land!"

Then a duck known as the hell-diver said, "My brother, you should have asked me before the others. Then you would have had land long ago. These ducks are my superiors in many ways, but they are poor divers."

The hell-diver plunged downward. He was gone a long time. When he came up, Old Man Coyote asked, "What luck have you had?"

"My brother, I have brought some soil," the hell-diver announced.

"Where?" Old Man Coyote asked eagerly.

The hell-diver had a little mud in his webbed feet.

"To every undertaking, there are four trials, but you have succeeded on your first try," Old Man Coyote said to the hell-diver. "Once I make the earth, you will flourish in ponds and streams. As for me, there is only one path—the path of the sun across the sky. Let us make the earth and let my path mark its boundaries."

Holding the mud in his hands, Old Man Coyote then started from the east, saying, "I will make the earth large with plenty of room for all the creatures." He traveled along on a westward journey, spreading the mud and making the earth.

When he was done, he declared, "Now that I have made the earth, there are many creatures that wish to come alive."

A wolf immediately howled in the east. Old Man Coyote then pointed toward the west, where there was another howl. "That was another coyote; he is my younger brother. He has attained life by his own great powers."

Old Man Coyote and the other coyote then took a walk onto the plains. "Look over there," Old Man Coyote said. "That is a human being. There are more of them. Come, let us look at him."

And this is how Old Man Coyote created the earth where the animals and people came to make their home.

The Cost of Trading

One of the strongest tribes of the Great Plains, the Crow became key traders in the area. With their horses, they expanded a trading network, which linked them to the eastern and western reaches of their territory. They most often traded horses but also acquired foods, such as salmon oil, **pemmican**, root flour, and berry cakes, and useful goods, such as sinew-backed bows, arrows, rope, clothing, shells, and greenstone for making pipes. They also exchanged buffalo robes and **buckskin** clothing for these objects, as well as Sioux **warbonnets** and pipes that they had previously obtained from tribes living to the east.

In 1805, while traveling to villages on the Missouri River, the Mountain Crow traded buffalo and deer skins with the Eastern Shoshone, who had Spanish saddles, metal axes, beads, and blankets. Thereafter, they traded regularly with the Eastern Shoshone and other tribes, east from the Missouri River and west to the Rocky

This war club was one of many different weapons the Crow used in battle.

Mountains. In 1806, the Crow encountered Meriwether Lewis and William Clark as they explored the recently acquired Louisiana Territory.

Soon after, many fur traders arrived in Crow territory and began to build forts and trading posts. Western traders brought iron kettles, metal knives, metal axes, guns, and cloth to the Crow in exchange for furs, especially beaver pelts. The Crow became a central tribe in the **fur trade**, trapping and trading more than other tribes. Because they prospered and had so many horses, the Crow were often attacked by the Cheyenne, Sioux, Arapaho, Blackfeet, and other tribes.

Guns obtained through trade helped in hunting but also intensified warfare among the Plains tribes. Battles had previously been contests of bravery, as warriors "**counted coup**," or got close enough to an enemy to touch him, but guns changed the way of warfare. Warriors could now shoot down their enemies from a great distance. As settlers pushed westward, the Crow came into greater conflict with other tribes, such as the Sioux, Cheyenne, and Blackfeet, who were displaced from their hunting grounds. The Crow fiercely battled these tribes as they struggled to protect their territory on the Great Plains.

After Europeans arrived, the Crow and other Native groups traded furs with them.

The Crow had many great leaders, including Chief Plenty Coups.

The People and Culture of the Crow

Facing Other Threats

In the latter part of the nineteenth century, the Crow faced one of the biggest threats to their nation: American settlers who wished to start new lives on fresh territory gained from the Louisiana Purchase. For over a hundred years, the Crow had thrived as hunters and warriors. However, by the 1850s, more settlers were pouring into their territory. Their great leader Chief Plenty Coups had a vision in which it was revealed to him that the Crow must cooperate with settlers and soldiers, otherwise their way of life would be lost forever. Over the centuries that followed, the Crow would endure hardship and obstacles related to the new people living in their land, but through it all, they would prevail.

Early Crow tribes traveled over grasslands, following herds of buffalo as they migrated.

CHAPTER TWO

[W]hen you know your language, your culture and traditions, it ... makes you unique.

—Dorothy Stops at Pretty Places, Crow Tribe member

BUILDING A CIVILIZATION

Before the arrival of Europeans and other settlers to the region, the Crow and their descendants formed intricate civilizations along the plains. Their everyday lives differed from other tribes in some ways and were similar in others. Their communities grew and flourished despite difficult weather conditions on the plains and other dangers and obstacles that faced them.

Migrations and the Importance of Horses

After the Crow migrated over the northern plains, they came to rely almost completely on the buffalo for food, clothing, and shelter. Following

The Crow continue to raise horses, which use pastures outside homes to graze.

the large herds, they hunted whenever they needed food or skins. These migrations usually followed the seasons. During the winter, bands camped along rivers. As spring approached, the men hunted deer, elk, bears, and pronghorns, as well as wild turkeys, prairie chickens, and rabbits. The women gathered the first

of the wild berries and fruits. The bands moved out to the plains again as the buffalo were fattening on the tender grass of spring.

After the Crow acquired horses, they quickly came to rely on these animals that enabled them to travel faster and farther. Men captured and broke wild **mustangs** but preferred to trade or capture horses that had already been broken. Stealing horses from an enemy tribe became a daring art among the Plains bands, including the Crow. A raid in which a warrior returned with many horses brought prestige and battle honors to him. Horses became a primary means of exchange, and giving horses away in ceremonies called **giveaways** was highly respected.

The Crow became expert riders—on bareback or with just a soft hide. Later, they became renowned for elaborate decorations for their horses, including fancy saddles. Women's saddles, in particular, had a Spanish design with very high projections in the front and back—called the pommel and cantle—which could reach as high as a rider's chest or shoulders. Men's saddles were not as tall. Eventually, the Spanish style was abandoned in favor of a two-cushion pad saddle. The Crow lavishly decorated every part of their horse's tack—pommel, cantle, bridle, stirrup, crupper, and even blankets. In the 1850s, the Crow began to place beaded collars on their mounts.

A family needed about ten horses: five as pack animals to carry or pull belongings and five for riding in hunting, warfare, and travel. Women packed the horses and the travois, which were used for carrying small children and those who were too ill or injured to ride horses. Horses carried the folded tipi cover and pulled the tipi poles. Women tied babies on **cradleboards** to saddle horns, while men strapped their shields and medicine bags to their saddles.

Constantly on the move, the Crow no longer planted corn or hunted small game. They preferred riding their horses after the buffalo herds instead of toiling in the fields or stalking game in the woods. In a single hunt, they could obtain enough meat to feed the band for months, as well as plenty of hides and bones for making tipis and tools. The Crow stored food, clothing, and other personal belongings in rawhide pouches called **parfleches** (par-FLESH-es).

If the herds continued to graze in the vicinity, the band might remain in one camp for several weeks, but generally, bands moved often, following the herds. Usually, the Crow made camp near streams and

The People and Culture of the Crow

This richly decorated parflech is used to store items such as buffalo meat or household objects.

woods, where they had a ready supply of fresh water for cooking and drinking, along with plenty of wood for their fires. Often at war with the other Plains tribes, especially the Cheyenne and Sioux, the Crow picked sites that could be easily defended against attack, often returning to a favorite camp year after year.

Family Dynamics

The Crow gathered in bands made up of family and **clan** members, each band with its own loosely defined territory. Families included not only the children and parents but also grandparents and unmarried aunts and uncles. Women, in particular, had many chores around the camp. They gathered plants, hauled firewood, carried water, cooked meals, tanned buffalo hides, made buckskin clothing, and sewed tipi coverings. They also set up and took down the tipis and cared for the children and the horses. Grandmothers often looked after the young children and helped with many of the chores around the tipi.

The number of Crow clans varied over time, but by 1877 there were thirteen: Prairie Dog, Bad Leggins, Skunk, Treacherous Lodges, Lost Lodges, Bad Honors, Butchers, Moving Lodges, Bear's Paw, Blackfoot Lodges, Fish Catchers, Antelope, and Raven. Each person belonged to the mother's clan, but was also considered a "child" of the father's clan. Everyone in the father's clan was regarded as a special parent to the child. The birth of a child joined the parents' two clans, which benefited the child. Clan fathers brought blessings to the child, which were obtained through dreams. In appreciation for these blessings, the mother's family hosted feasts for the father and presented him with gifts, such as **moccasins**, beadwork, buffalo robes, and horses. Fathers usually had several of these dream blessings, which were used in naming children, honoring a boy who killed his first deer or buffalo, or marking another occasion of good fortune. Fathers could include other men in the clan, not just a child's biological father. Children could also have adopted medicine fathers, who offered instruction in religious ceremonies and provided medicine bundles or other sacred objects to their "sons." The sharing of sacred power and protection of wealth in the clan and band was further strengthened in the giveaway.

Viewing themselves as brothers and sisters, clan members were expected to work together, avenge

Women decorated moccasins with beads and feathers.

crimes against relatives, and mourn deaths of their members. They also arranged marriages among clan members. Two or three clans often formed groups called **phratries** that cooperated in hunting, feasting, and other activities. The Crow believed that people who had grown up together worked better as a group. Mutual respect, cooperation, and understanding ensured safety and success in the dangerous tasks of hunting and warfare. Even small raids to steal horses usually included several closely related men—fathers, sons, and brothers. Similarly, related women—mothers, daughters, and sisters—worked better on cooperative tasks, such as preserving stores of meat, tanning buffalo hides, and making tipi covers. One of the worst insults was to say, "You are without relatives."

Living in small bands, the Crow had no social classes and did not need a complicated system of governing themselves. Family and clan members relied primarily on ridicule and gossip to punish anyone who broke the rules. It was a man's prowess as a hunter and warrior and a woman's ability in providing for her family that mattered most to the members of the band. Strength and skill were essential for survival out on the open plains, although generosity was also admired. A wealthy man with many horses enjoyed prestige, but he was expected to share his food and belongings with others in giveaways.

People did belong to a variety of groups, including military, religious, and curing societies. Men could also belong to a society based on their wealth, which was determined by the number of horses they owned. Most of the able-bodied men in the band were members of one of the military societies. The most famous of these groups were highly regarded for their bravery and prowess as warriors. These societies maintained order in the band, in addition to fighting in battles.

Each clan had its own leaders, or chiefs, who achieved their status based on their wealth, courage, intelligence, and medicine powers. These men formed a council of elders, in which they smoked a sacred pipe, offered prayers, and sought consensus on a decision. However, these chiefs had no authority in settling murders and other disputes between families and clans. Along with the chiefs, the members of the warrior societies also occupied an honored position, and the chiefs often consulted with them, even on matters of peace.

War Societies

Between ages fourteen and sixteen, young men joined the Hammer Owners, a young men's group similar to the men's war societies. Young members served as water boys or messengers on war parties. Eager to prove themselves in battle, young men looked forward to an invitation to join one of the men's military societies, which included the Kitfox, Lumpwood, Big Dog, Muddy Hand, Bull Owner, Long Crazy Dog, Crazy Dog Who Wishes to Die, Half-Shaved Head, Muddy Mouth, and Little Dog. However, by the late 1800s, the Crow had only four main societies: Lumpwood, Fox, Muddy Hand, and Big Dog.

Crow warriors sit on horseback atop a hill.

These societies shared power with chiefs, and one was chosen each year to serve as camp police known as **Akíssatre**. This society mediated personal conflicts in the camp, organized band migrations, and oversaw buffalo hunts. It was essential that lone hunters not stampede the herd, so the society had the authority to capture and punish any violators by whipping them, killing their horses, and taking away the buffalo they had hunted. When an old warrior retired, he became an honored member of the Bull Owners society. Because of his long years of experience, his counsel was often sought at public gatherings.

Ambitious young men strove to become leaders of war parties. Known as pipe holders, they were entitled to wear shirts of ermine strips and scalps. No one had to join a war party, but if a leader had proven himself and if dreams seemed to favor him with powerful medicine, other warriors were eager to ride with him. Leaders of war parties might then rise to the ranks of chiefs known as *wace-ícce* (pronounced wuh-chay-ITCH-cheh), which means "good men."

Running the Clan

One man in the band served as the head chief known as *aswace-icce*. A chief had to prove himself in four brave deeds: leading a raid that took scalps or horses without loss of Crow life, capturing a horse picketed in an enemy camp, seizing a weapon from an enemy warrior, and being the first man in a war party to count coup. The head chief also had to be a generous man who had powerful medicine and ability as a speaker and storyteller. The chief maintained order in the band and decided when the band would break camp, when they would go on a buffalo hunt, and if they would go to war. He usually consulted with the elders on important decisions and with medicine men, or **shamans**, to decide upon a hunt. Scouts were then sent out to find the herds of buffalo. When the camp was migrating, the chief was called "he leads the moving band." The chief carried a sacred pipe and led the procession to the next campsite—and no one was allowed to go before him. If a chief failed to defend and provide for the band, he would be replaced by another warrior.

Housing and Shelter

When the Crow were part of the Hidatsa people and made their home in the Dakotas, they lived in earth

Tipis continue to hold a symbolic and traditional meaning for Crow people.

lodges like the other Hidatsa people and their closely related neighbors, the Mandan. However, as they migrated to Montana and began to hunt buffalo, they adopted the tipi. Made of wooden poles and stitched buffalo hides, these practical shelters were well suited to their nomadic way of life. Working together, several women could easily set up or take down a tipi in a matter of minutes. The Crow used the disassembled tipi poles as a travois to carry the buffalo-hide covering and their belongings from one camp to another. The poles were strapped to a horse's shoulders, with the other end dragging on the ground. On the rough ground of the open prairie, the travois worked better than wheels. Tipis varied in size—they could stand 25 feet (7.6 meters) tall or higher. Their coverings were made of seven to twenty tanned buffalo hides. A large tipi could shelter as many as forty people, but usually about twelve family members lived in one of these lodges.

To make tipis, the men journeyed into the hills to cut down long, slender pine trees for lodge poles. The bark was stripped and the strong, light poles were dried in the sun, then hauled back to the camp. To raise a tipi, women lashed four of the poles together, which formed the "foundation" for the frame. Lifting and spreading out the bottom ends of the poles, they stood the cone-shaped frame upright. They then laid ten to twenty-five smaller poles around the four main poles.

To make the covering, women stretched and staked fresh, or "green," buffalo hides on the ground and scraped off the fat and flesh with sharp-bladed tools made from bones or antlers. They let the hides dry in the sun and then scraped off the coarse brown hair. Women then tanned the stiff hides by smearing a mixture of buffalo fat, brains, and liver on both sides. They alternately rubbed the hides, rinsed them in water, and then laboriously kneaded them. Tanning softened and whitened the hides.

Several hides then had to be sewn into a tipi covering. This was a challenging task and the women relied on a skilled lodge cutter to oversee the making of the covering. Under her direction, several women laid out seven to twenty tanned buffalo hides, fitted them like pieces of a puzzle, and carefully stitched them together to make a covering. The covering, which was often decorated with paintings and **quillwork**, was attached to a pole and raised, then drawn around the cone-shaped frame.

Held together with wooden pins, the covering had two wing-shaped flaps at the top, which were turned back to form a smoke hole or closed to keep out the rain. The tipi also had a U-shaped doorway, which was covered with a hide flap and adorned with rawhide thongs, porcupine quills, feathers, or horsetails. The doorway always faced east—away from the prevailing wind and toward the rising sun. Seeking powerful medicine, a man would step forth at daybreak and offer a prayer to the sun.

During a summer heat wave, the bottom edges of the tipi could be raised to allow a cool breeze through the dwelling. In the winter, however, the Crow often banked the tipi with a **berm**, or sloped earthen wall, for better insulation. They also hung a "dew cloth" made of buffalo hides on the inside walls from about shoulder-height down to the ground. Decorated with paintings of battles, dreams, and visions, the dew cloth kept out dampness and created pockets of insulating air. With a fire burning in the center of the earthen floor and buffalo robes lining the walls, tipis stayed warm throughout the coldest months.

Women owned the tipis and kept stews and soups simmering in their cooking pots. Pouches of belongings and stored food lined the inside walls. Furnishings included backrests and buffalo robes. Buffalo-hide screens, depicting a warrior's heroic deeds, separated sleeping spaces and shielded the fire from draft. People slept along the inside walls of the tipi.

The Crow also covered poles with buffalo hides to make small dome-shaped **sweat lodges**. Inside the sweat lodges, men poured water over heated rocks and purified themselves in the rising steam.

Socializing

The Crow liked to get together with others in the camp, often over a meal, and a buffalo meat stew or other hearty dish was always simmering in a pot over the fire. Gathering in the tipi, people played games, told stories, or spoke proudly of their deeds of skill and courage. Boasting was encouraged because warriors had to be strong and brave to hunt buffalo, defeat their enemies, and endure the cold winters. While visiting, men often enjoyed a smoke. The aroma of tobacco wafted through the lodge as the pipe was handed from one man to another.

When they got together, the Crow especially liked to play guessing games, such as the hand game. In this game, players hid elk-tooth counters in their hands. Women enjoyed dice games in which they tossed marked sticks or bounced plum stones in a bowl, trying to turn up the painted sides. In the spring, women also played shinny, which was similar to field hockey, with a curved wooden stick and a hide ball stuffed with animal hair. Men took part in archery competitions with bows and arrows, and they threw spears at rolling hoops. They loved to compete in foot and horse races. In the winter, the men's societies competed in sliding and pushing contests on the ice. Boys and young men threw buffalo ribs across the ice in a game called snow snake. They also pulled their girlfriends on sleds and coasted down hills on toboggans made of buffalo ribs and hides. Boys spun cone-shaped tops on the ice. Whatever the season, the Crow liked to work and play together with others in their family, clan, and band.

The Crow consider the sun the supreme being in their religion.

Throughout their early years, the Crow lived off the land. They respected it and treated it kindly. Their lifestyle was undisturbed for centuries. As the Crow communities advanced, they formed connections with tribes and eventually with settlers. This was not always easy and often led to conflict. However, the Crow proved time and time again they were determined to remain a prominent culture in western North America.

The Crow uphold their religious beliefs by making and displaying sacred objects.

CHAPTER THREE

To be a Crow Indian is to be connected to the land.

—Linda Pease,
Crow Tribe member

LIFE IN THE CROW NATION

As a result of their communities, the Crow developed a number of traditions and personal beliefs regarding life and death. Similarly, they formed habits and practices concerning warfare and everyday chores. These traditions were passed down from generation to generation.

The Life Cycle

One of the first traditions passed down concerned the life cycle. To the Crow, all life was sacred and should be respected. The human life cycle was filled with many nurturing tribal traditions intended to promote an attitude of respect.

A mother looks fondly on her child, strapped in a cradleboard.

Life Begins

When a woman was about to give birth, she was assisted by a grandmother or one or more older, experienced women who served as midwives. The woman knelt on a pile of robes and grasped two poles set up over where her pillow was placed when she slept. Men were not allowed in the lodge while she was in labor. After the birth, a midwife cut the umbilical cord, leaving about three inches. The baby was then washed, greased, snugly wrapped in a soft robe, and placed in a cradleboard with moss for a diaper. The mother nursed the baby whenever it was hungry. Except for cleaning, the infant spent most of the day in the cradleboard, which the mother hung on a lodgepole or leaned against the tipi as she worked about the camp. The baby could watch her cooking at the fire or tanning buffalo hides. If the camp moved, the mother fastened the cradleboard to her saddle or travois pole. The baby remained in the cradleboard until it was old enough to sit up on its own.

Two days after it was born, the baby had its ears pierced. On the fourth day, a clan elder brought the infant under the protection of his medicine, lifting the baby three times in sacred cedar smoke and on the fourth time naming it after a dream or coup. When the child took its first steps, the father then gave a horse to the namer.

Growing Up

The Crow doted upon their children, who were rarely punished but gently encouraged to be well behaved. The mother's brother acted as an older brother or father to her sons. He helped the boy get his first horse and saddle, watched over him on raids, and taught him proper conduct for a Crow man. Similarly, a mother's sisters acted as mothers to her sons and daughters.

Children were taught to be generous with others and especially respectful of elders. From an early age, children were allowed a great deal of independence. Yet parents expected boys to strive to become skilled hunters and warriors. Similarly, girls were expected to learn all the skills needed to care for a family.

At an early age, boys were given small bows and arrows to practice shooting at birds and small game. Playing with dolls and small tipis, girls learned to manage households. As soon as they were able to walk, girls followed their mothers, fetching wood and water. Over time, they learned how to cook meals, do fancy

A young member
of the Crow Nation

quillwork, tan buffalo hides, and undertake many other
tasks around the camp.

Both girls and boys learned to ride horses not long
after they took their first steps. Soon after he learned
to ride, a boy helped out on a buffalo hunt. While
he served as a water boy or fire keeper, he observed
how the men hunted. The children had to strengthen
their bodies if they were going to survive a hard life as
hunters, warriors, and gatherers. To strengthen their
bodies, both girls and boys competed in races on
foot and on horseback and played vigorous games of
running and jumping.

Despite the intense competition of their games,
children got along well. They were expected to be

cheerful and cooperative with each other. Children sometimes set up a "play camp" not far from their bands' tipis. The girls raised lodge poles, took care of the young children, and prepared meals. Riding sticks that served as horses, the boys pretended to hunt buffalo and go to war.

During the winter months, children gathered around their elders and listened to stories about the creation of the Crow and the deeds of Old Man Coyote. Through these stories, children learned of the history and customs of their people in the hopes that someday they too would pass on these customs and beliefs to their own children.

Buffalo graze on the
National Bison Range in Montana.

A young woman dressed in traditional Crow clothing

The People and Culture of the Crow

Entering Adulthood

When he was about twelve years old, a young man was expected to begin to prove himself as a hunter and warrior, since he would be needed to provide for his family and defend the band. Around this time, he might join the men as a buffalo hunter. If he was able to kill a calf, his father held a feast in his honor and gave away one of his finest horses to another member of the band. It was an important turning point in the youth's life. If he continued to do well on buffalo hunts, he would be asked to join a war party.

A young man went on a vision quest in hopes of finding a guardian spirit. He first purified himself with a sweat bath, then journeyed to a sacred place in the mountains. There he fasted and slept uncovered in the cold for three nights. He might also cut off strips of his own flesh and perhaps a finger joint as a sacrifice to the spirits. After he had prayed and made these brave sacrifices, a guardian spirit hopefully appeared to him on the fourth day. This spirit helper revealed a sacred song and symbols that the youth could use in calling for help in the future. A young man might also seek a vision at a Sun Dance in which he cut two slits in his chest and ran wooden skewers through the wounds. The skewers were tied to a pole, and the young man leaned away from a pole until his flesh tore away. In his deep pain, the young man received a vision.

As she grew up, a young woman was carefully watched by her mother, aunts, and grandmothers. These women advised her to remain close to the lodge fire and not to wander about the camp. When she had her first menstrual period, a girl told her mother.

Thereafter, during every period, she had to sleep in a special lodge in the camp.

Marrying

Traditionally, couples courted in secret. A young man might play a wooden flute to call a young woman to meet with him. Brothers had a strong influence in a girl's life. Young women were taught not to shame their brothers by having children out of wedlock. Older brothers also had the right to approve of their sister's choice for a mate. If an older brother opposed a marriage, the couple sometimes eloped. When a couple wanted to be married, older women relatives determined how many horses the groom should offer as payment for his bride. The groom then offered horses to the woman's brothers and meat to her mother.

Since many warriors lost their lives in battle, there were often fewer men than women in a camp, so a man might have two or more wives. These wives were often sisters. If a man's wife

A Crow warrior named Hoop on the Forehead looks over his village.

died soon after marriage, he was often offered one of her sisters as another wife. If he had several wives, the husband had to be able to provide for his large family.

After a couple had married, sisters-in-law and brothers-in-law respected each other and often presented each other with gifts. These bonds helped to strengthen family relationships within the band. A man also respected his mother-in-law and father-in-law by not touching, speaking to, staring at, or eating with either of them.

If a couple did not get along, divorce was possible. For most couples, however, marriage was viewed as a lifetime commitment.

Dying

Whether a man died in battle or a woman of old age, the person was expected to face the moment with courage. If a young warrior was killed by an enemy, the entire camp mourned. The body was placed on view and everyone was invited to visit and smoke with their brave friend. Overcome with grief, people cut their hair. Women pierced the skin of their heads with arrowheads. The wife, mother, and often the sisters slashed their legs with knives. Sometimes, they chopped off a fingertip or joint.

Entering a period of deep mourning, the family prepared the body for its final resting place. The deceased was dressed in his or her finest clothing, then wrapped in the upper part of a tipi covering. People sang and prayed over the body. The bundle was carried from the tipi, but never from the main entrance for fear that the ghost of the departed would come back and take another member of the household. Mourners never mentioned the deceased directly. They would say, "He is not here."

Early in their history, the Crow buried the dead in rock shelters or caves. They began to place bodies on scaffolds and in trees around 1825. A chief was laid to rest on a four-pole scaffold in a tipi adorned with red stripes and scalps. Decorated with wolf skins, his lance was placed outside the doorway along with the manes and tails of his favorite horses.

The deceased's tipi and personal belongings were given away, along with gifts from the members of his warrior society. Close relatives mourned the death of their loved one for a year or until an enemy had been killed.

War and Hunting

The Crow were almost continually at war with the Cheyenne, Sioux, and Blackfeet who shared their hunting grounds. Warfare among the Plains tribes was a dangerous venture. A warrior could easily get killed, which added to the risk of battle, but despite the honor that came from heroic or daring acts, warriors valued their lives. In victory, a chief was shamed if he lost even one man in his party. For young warriors, the main reason for going into battle was counting coup. Warriors counted coup by getting close enough to physically touch an enemy. To shoot an enemy from a distance was not as heroic as riding up and actually striking a foe.

Their primary weapons included bows and arrows, war clubs, knives, spears, war shields, and, later, firearms. Men also carried their medicine bundle and

The People and Culture of the Crow

pipe for calling on the spirits for protection. Before going on a raid, however, the warriors awaited a dream, which foretold a victory. Just before engaging the enemy in a raid, the leader of a war party sought his medicine to confirm the promised vision of success. Horse raids were often led by a man with blackbird medicine, who attached the skins of this bird to his head. The leader took charge of the raid, including the distribution of the horses and loot from the attack.

Led by an experienced warrior known for his courage, skill, and good luck, war parties raided camps to steal horses—another way of counting coup—or to avenge a relative who had been killed by an enemy. Raiding parties were usually small, but revenge expeditions under a great chief might have several hundred warriors. In revenge killings, Crow warriors sometimes mutilated the dead by cutting off the heads and raising them on poles. They also raised enemy scalps on poles, and the mourners all joined in a victory dance.

The northern plains abounded in big game, including deer, elk, bighorn sheep, and grizzly bears. However, the Crow relied mostly on the buffalo, which they hunted in several different ways. Occasionally, a man stalked and killed a single animal with a bow and arrows. Other times, a small hunting party rushed down on a few grazing buffalo. However, most often, the Crow planned large communal hunts that included the entire band. Men were not allowed to hunt alone at this time, because they might stampede the herd. In a group hunt, men drove herds over a cliff or into a narrow canyon where they could be trapped and easily killed.

RECICPE

CHOKE-CHERRY PUDDING

INGREDIENTS

2 cups (473 milliliters) fresh, frozen, canned, or dried
 chokecherries (may substitute tart pie cherries)

2 cups (473 mL) water [about 4 cups (946 mL) for dried
 cherries]

Honey or sugar to taste

2 tablespoons (30 mL) arrowroot or 0.25 cups (59 mL)
 flour

Combine the chokecherries and water in a saucepan.
Cover and cook, stirring frequently, over medium heat until
the cherries become soft and juicy. Sweeten the mixture
with honey or sugar to taste. In a small bowl, combine the
arrowroot or flour with enough water to make a thin creamy
liquid. Gradually stir this liquid into the cherry mixture and
simmer, stirring frequently, until thickened. The pudding
may be served by itself or with fry bread. Serves four to six.

Only the men hunted buffalo, but after the hunt, the women had hard work to do. They skinned and butchered the many large animals strewn all over the plains. Everyone in the band shared the meat—giving was very important to the Crow, especially for those who were the ablest hunters and warriors. The liver and other organs that quickly spoiled in the summer heat were cooked and eaten right away, as well as the tongue, hump meat, and ribs. Most of the fresh meat was then packed on travois and hauled back to camp.

Cooking

Along with tanning hides and making tipis, Crow women prepared all the meals for their families. When they were living in the Dakotas, they grew corn, beans, and squash, but after moving west, they abandoned farming and primarily relied on buffalo. Their diet of buffalo meat was supplemented by prairie turnips and a little corn that they obtained through trade with other tribes. Women dug up prairie turnips with digging sticks, about 2.5 feet (0.8 m) long and padded with buffalo hair and leather. They also gathered fruits, seeds, nuts, berries, and other roots. When the Crow began to trade with American settlers, they added coffee, sugar, and flour to their foodstuffs.

Most buffalo meat was thinly sliced, hung over poles, and dried in the sun. Smoke from the fires under the drying racks helped to preserve the meat and give it a good flavor. With stones, women pounded some of this dried meat, or jerky, into a coarse powder. They mixed the pounded meat with fat and dried fruits and berries, especially chokecherries, to make pemmican.

Women stored pemmican in parfleches for later use when other foods were scarce. Men also ate pemmican on long journeys.

Dried meat and pemmican could be eaten without cooking, but meat was most often boiled in soups or stews or roasted over a fire. The Crow started fires with a wooden stick called a fire drill. Between the palms of their hands, they rapidly twirled a sagebrush or wild grape drill against a cottonwood plank with dried bark or powdered buffalo dung as tinder. The friction generated enough heat to light the tinder. Once a fire was started, women used **buffalo chips** as fuel—and as punks for carrying hot coals from one camp to another. Women often set up a hide windbreak or small tipi for cooking meals, as well as for working hides and sewing clothes. To boil food, women dug a pit in the ground, which they lined with animal skins or a buffalo stomach. They filled the makeshift pot with water then dropped in heated stones until their meat and vegetables were boiled.

Sitting around the campfire, people ate with wooden bowls made from box elder and spoons, dishes, and cups made from the horns of mountain sheep and buffalo. The horns were first softened in hot water and then shaped into useful forms. People also used buffalo shoulder blades as dishes.

Clothes and Accessories

Women made all the clothing for their families from tanned deer, elk, antelope, or bighorn sheep hides. They usually adorned this buckskin clothing with fringes on the seams and dyed porcupine quills. They first dyed the hollow quills and cut them into short pieces, then they carefully sewed them onto the garment. When the Crow encountered European traders, they acquired glass beads, which they used instead of quills.

Among the Plains tribes, Crow men were renowned for their elaborate clothing, which was often decorated with pictures that depicted the heroic deeds of a warrior's life. During warm weather, men wore only fringed **breechcloths** and moccasins made from soft buckskin. As the cold winds of the northern plains swept down upon them, they put on hip-length buckskin leggings with long fringe and wide flaps at the bottom. Leggings were decorated with painted stripes, a rectangular patch at the bottom, and quill-wrapped horsehair fringe. Distinguished warriors could wear leggings trimmed with hair locks. Men wore knee-length shirts with attached sleeves, which were adorned with ornate quill and bead designs, especially bands on the sleeves and shoulders. The sleeves were often fringed with long twists of buckskin, ermine tails, or hair bundles. Warriors occasionally trimmed their war shirts with the scalps of their enemies. Sometimes shirts were pointed at the lower edge front and back, like those of subarctic tribes that lived to the north of the Crow. These points were often tipped with ermine tails. Men often attached medicine bags and eagle feathers to their shirts.

Because they worked hard around the camp, the women did not wear as neat and fancy clothing as the men. Originally, they wore a wraparound buckskin skirt with a buckskin poncho in cool weather. However, they adopted Plains-style calf-length, fringed dresses made of two skins from deer or mountain sheep sewn together. These ankle-length dresses were longer than those of neighboring tribes and often worn with a belt. Women often fringed their dresses and trimmed them with ermine, quillwork, and, later, glass beads. But they were renowned for their elk-teeth dresses, which were adorned with concentric arcs of elk teeth on the front and back—about three hundred and sometimes as many as a thousand elk teeth on one dress. One hundred elk teeth could buy a good horse, so these were expensive dresses. They also applied patches at the sides of the bottom of the dress. The umbilical cord of a girl was kept in a bag and when she was old enough to wear an elk-teeth dress, the bag was tied at the back. Women also wore buckskin leggings and moccasins, which were painted and adorned with fringes and quillwork. In later years, they came to decorate leggings with rows of blue beads.

Soft-soled moccasins were made of one piece of buckskin with side seams, but the Crow later adopted the hard-soled style of the Plains tribes. Women often decorated moccasins with stripes on the front, especially red and green, along with bold geometric designs on solid-color backgrounds. The Crow also liked a keyhole design and what was known as the "Blackfoot U" on the instep. When a warrior had counted coup, he could attach wolf tails to the heels of his moccasins.

Warriors also wore warbonnets of eagle feathers and may have invented this style of headdress. However, they more often wore a high-crown headdress in which a circlet of feathers was attached to a leather brow band. They also wore a headdress of buffalo horns or

Ornately decorated Crow moccasins, circa 1940

antelope horns with long trails of feathers attached.
Sometimes, they wore a headdress made of an entire
eagle or other large bird. In the summer, they wore
rawhide visors to shade against the intense sun. In the

winter, the Crow wore fur mittens and caps. Both men and women wrapped themselves in robes made of elk or thick buffalo hides. These robes featured bold designs, such as a feathered circle, hourglass, triangle, and other symbols. They also liked to decorate robes with strips of quillwork.

Men, especially chiefs, carried large eagle-feather fans. People also wore buckskin belts, often with the long ends split and hanging loose, painted in a distinctive Crow style—with rectangles, diamonds, hourglasses, triangles, and other bold shapes. They also wore bags and pouches that were painted rather than decorated with quillwork or beadwork. These bags held small personal objects, such as paints, sewing equipment, and tobacco. They also made decorated leather sheaths for knives and awls.

Both men and women wore jewelry, but men especially liked dangling earrings, bear-claw necklaces, and strings of shells, beads, and elk or deer teeth. Although the Crow did not have special ear-piercing ceremonies like other tribes, they pierced their ears and wore shell and quill jewelry. Some women adorned themselves with strings of earrings made from bluish-green abalone shells and polished disks cut from the shoulder blade of a buffalo.

Crow men were especially proud of their very long hair, which they often lengthened by gluing on additional locks of horsehair or human hair, especially from women who had cut their hair in mourning. Their hair often reached the ground, and the hair of Chief Long Hair was believed to be 10 feet (3 m) long. His hair was wound in a wrap and folded in a container, which he carried with him. He believed that the hair was his "medicine." Men wore their long hair in various styles—loose, pompadour, topknot, forelocks, bangs, braids, and many little braids. They sometimes attached "Crow bows" to braids on either side of the head. They used a heated stick as a curling iron and smeared bear

Many Crow men grew their hair very long. This warrior's hair stretches all the way down his back.

grease on their hair to stiffen it. Cactus pith gave their hair a glossy sheen, and castoreum and sweetgrass were used to perfume it. Men often further decorated their hair with beaded bows, heavy strings of beads or shells, and feathers.

Crow women wore their hair hanging loose or in two braids. Their hair was usually short since it had to be pulled out or cut during times of mourning. By the late 1840s, women wore their hair long, often to the shoulders, with bangs in the front. They painted a line along the part with red ocher. They tied their hair at night so that it did not become tangled.

Both men and women tattooed themselves. This was done by pricking the skin with a porcupine quill and rubbing powered charcoal into the small wound. Men favored lines on their chins, a dot on the nose, and a circle on the forehead, although women more often tattooed themselves. Men also painted their faces and bodies. Painting the face black meant that the warrior was going to avenge a death. However, they most often painted red designs on their faces and a tinge of yellow paint on their eyelids. They painted horizontal stripes on their chests and arms as symbols of their war exploits.

By the 1850s, felt hats were replacing feather headdresses. Crow women were making cloth dresses, breechcloths, and leggings patterned after traditional buckskin styles. They favored red, green, and especially blue cloth. As the buffalo vanished, they also traded for striped Mackinaw woolen blankets, which they used instead of buffalo robes or made into coats. All of these garments were heavily decorated with beadwork.

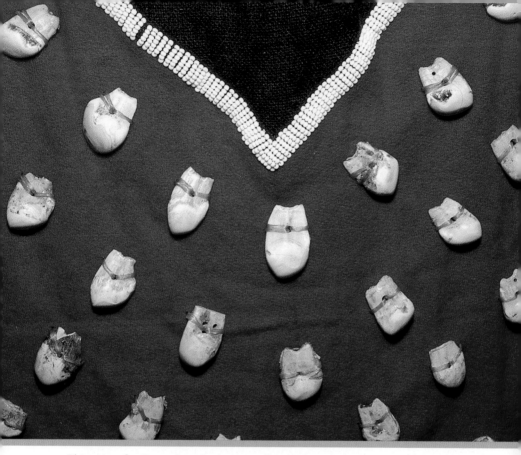

This part of a Crow dress is decorated with elk teeth.

Arts and Crafts

The Crow made and used clay pottery and woven baskets before they moved out onto the plains. However, like other Plains tribes, they abandoned these handicrafts in favor of parfleches and other leather goods, which were decorated with colorful paintings or intricate quillwork. The Crow were especially noted for their finely crafted parfleches, clothing, blankets, and weapons.

Because of their nomadic way of life, the Crow needed household goods that were light and durable, so they could be carried easily to the next camp. Pottery was not only heavy but it could be broken on their long journeys. However, food, clothing, and other personal belongings could be safely tucked in leather parfleches of different sizes. The stiff, rectangular pouches were beautifully painted with bold rectangles and triangles, traditionally in red, blue, and green.

Leather for parfleches usually came from the buffalo, as did the material for many other handicrafts. In fact, the horns, hides, and bones of a single buffalo provided many useful tools and household items. The Crow made knives, scrapers, and needles from the bones. Bones were also fashioned into smoking pipes and children's toys. Horns were used to make spoons, cups, and ladles. The women turned hides into tipi covers, robes, blankets, clothing, and moccasins. Rawhide was made into drums and the thick neck skin was shaped into tough war shields. The hooves were made into rattles, and even the tail made an excellent flyswatter. Rawhide strips could be woven into sturdy ropes, and sinew was used as sewing thread. The Crow cooked meat and vegetables in the lining of a buffalo paunch, or stomach. A buffalo paunch could also be used as a water pot, and the bladder, once rinsed and dried, made an excellent canteen.

The Crow made wood bows from ash and hickory and arrow shafts from chokecherry. Expert craftsmen straightened the shaft with grooved stones or a mountain sheep horn. They also made strong bows of layers of elk and sheep horn that were spliced and glued with bands of tough sinew from the neck and shoulders of buffalo. Men made quivers for holding arrows from the skins of otters, mountain sheep, or buffalo calves. Men also made deadly war lances that were decorated with feathers and war shields of tough buffalo rawhide. Warriors often prayed to the spirits who lent powerful medicine to their lances and other weapons, especially war shields. Warriors decorated their shields with striking and colorful designs of fierce bears, buffalo bulls, storm clouds, and lightning that symbolized these spirits.

In addition to these weapons and tools, the Crow made fire drills, stone scrapers, and other handy objects. They made beautiful cradleboards that were U-shaped at the top and tapered at the bottom. Backrests used in the tipi were made of willow sticks bound with sinew and hung on a tripod of wooden poles.

All of these light, portable tools, weapons, and household items helped the Crow to live comfortably both in camp and on the trail as they journeyed over the plains.

The Crow's way of life changed when Europeans and other settlers set up communities inside their territory. Prior to their arrival, and for many years following, however, the Crow's culture was unique and full of innovation, structure, and support. As shown, the Crow had many traditions that made them stand out among other Plains tribes.

The scenery of Montana inspired many Crow stories.

CHAPTER FOUR

Being a Crow means being spiritual.

—Anna DeCrane,
Crow Tribe member

BELIEFS OF THE CROW

As with many other cultures, the Crow had extensive belief systems. Their religious practices influenced many parts of their lives and brought people together. Their beliefs were passed down through word of mouth, often through telling stories about the gods and other spirits that formed the basis of their religion.

The Crow hunted many animals for food or sacrifice, including blacktail deer.

Hierarchy of the Gods

Like other Plains tribes, the Crow believed that the sun, whom they addressed as Father and Old Man Coyote, was the most powerful supernatural being. People fasted and offered sacrifices to the sun. They also prayed to many other spirits, especially First Maker, The One Above, Morning Star, Buffalo, Thunderbird, Eagle, and Dwarf People. The Crow believed that Old Man Coyote created the earth, along with First Man, First Woman, and a flock of crows. He then placed the Crow people in their homeland on the Yellowstone River and surrounded them with hostile tribes against whom they were destined to continually wage war. Old Man Coyote then struck a tree and white men came out of a hole like mice, but he told the Crow not to fight these people, who would teach them how to make iron.

　　　　　The People and Culture of the Crow

Old Man Coyote told the people to pray to him and make offerings of white buffalo hides, blacktail deer skins, and white tail hawk feathers. In return, Old Man Coyote promised to help the Crow people.

Spirits

The Crow believed that some spirits had evil intentions, and people had to call upon powerful medicine to defeat them. In fact, much of Crow religion was based on spiritual power, or medicine, which was necessary if one was to prosper in life. This supernatural medicine, which went well beyond human ability, came from spirit helpers or guardian spirits. In a vision quest or sacred sweat, a person fasted and offered sacrifices in hopes that a spirit helper would come to him. The spirit helper would give him rights to medicine, including songs, body painting, and sacred objects to be kept in a medicine bundle. The vision seeker thought of the spirit as a "father," just as he might borrow medicine from a clan father. He could do so four times, then he had to repay the spirit with horses, choice portions of buffalo meat, and other wealth, after which he then owned the medicine. Rights to the medicine were usually revealed in a dream or vision.

The Crow relied on medicine bundles in both private and public ceremonies to insure prosperity, good health, and long life. The medicine bundles also helped the band flourish and win victories over its enemies. Religious practices were spread among medicine bundle owners, groups of those who owned the same medicine, and society members who had purchased rights to certain medicines. For example,

Crow warriors wore medicine charms, such as this one, to help give them strength during battle.

the Cooked Meat Singing ceremony brought together people who owned **rock medicines**—small stones kept as charms, or amulets, believed to have sacred power—while the Bear Song dancers gathered to portray the mysterious spirit that lived within each person. Other medicine societies included the Tobacco, Horse Dance, and Sacred Pipe. Each had special powers, but all promised good fortune in health, war, and wealth. Of these, the Tobacco society was the most renowned. No Vitals, who led the Crow when they separated from the Hidatsa, received the gift of tobacco at Devils Lake in eastern North Dakota. It was believed that Morning Star transformed himself from a human into tobacco at the creation. The spirits told the Crow to grow and worship this sacred plant, which shaped their destiny as a people.

When they died, the Crow believed that their souls journeyed to a camp that resembled life on earth. However, some souls became ghosts, who appeared as whirlwinds or called like owls in the night. Ghosts might curse a person by stealing a lock of hair or bless someone with a vision. Some shamans had ghost powers, which enabled them to find lost persons or belongings.

Shamans

The Crow had two kinds of shamans. One kind was a healer who treated minor illnesses and injuries with herbal medicines. These healers might wrap a salve on a wound or lance a swollen finger. The other kind of shamans were medicine men or women, who had spiritual powers to treat evil curses, serious illnesses, and other afflictions, such as a bite from a poisonous snake. Shamans might ritually suck the evil out of a patient and spit it on the ground in hopes of curing the sickness. They also blew whistles, beat on drums, and shook gourd rattles, as well as offering prayers during their healing rituals. Considered the voice of the spirits, the drum figured prominently in ceremonies. Its round shape symbolized the universe, and its steady beat symbolized the pulsing heart. It comforted patients in body and in mind.

Celebrations and Religious Practices

The Crow most often held ceremonies in the fall and spring. In September or October, after a rock medicine owner had received instructions in a dream, guests were invited to a feast called the Cooked Meat Singing. At this event, people expressed their joy at the bounty of buffalo meat. They prayed that the next year would also be happy and plentiful. In the Bear Song, dancers showed their medicine power for the next year by

A medicine man wears
an eagle on his head.

A vision quest often involved piercing a person's skin and stretching it.

taking items from their mouths—horse and buffalo tails, bear teeth, and eggs. In the spring, people gathered for the tobacco planting, followed by adoption rites. The spring thunder announced the reawakening of the earth for another year—and time to open medicine bundles during full moon ceremonies.

The most sacred Crow rituals were the Sacred Sweat, the Tobacco Ceremony, and the Sun Dance, which were held in late spring and summer—usually for healing or revenge. A man hosted a Sun Dance in hopes of receiving a special vision to cure a sick child or avenge a murder. Called a whistler, the host asked for the help of a shaman who had a powerful Sun Dance bundle. The whistler and people placed themselves under the direction of the owner of this bundle, which held a sacred doll, or manikin. The whistler danced before the manikin, which was displayed in a hoop adorned with eagle feathers and tied to a cedar tree. He danced on a bed of white clay and blew prayer wishes through his eagle-bone whistle. Other men who sought visions could participate in the Sun Dance by fasting, piercing themselves, or dragging buffalo skulls in hope of receiving medicine power through a vision. When the whistler saw the manikin turn black, he knew that his revenge had been granted and the Sun Dance ended. For a time, the US government outlawed the Sun Dance, but it was revived in 1941 by William Big Day. The Crow continue to hold two or three Sun Dances every summer.

Telling Stories

The Crow listened reverently to stories about the deeds of Old Man Coyote and other spiritual heroes. Through these stories, they learned about their beliefs and rituals that had been passed down through the generations. Telling a story was often a sacred act. Here is a story about how the Crow came to respect their most important religious ceremonies:

A long time ago there were four brothers among the Crow who grew up to become men. One of them suggested, "We are going to undertake four different rituals."

One was going to pray and make an offering to the Sun every morning. The second was to go out for one, two, three, or four days

Many Native American groups, including the Crow, passed down the history and beliefs of their people through storytelling.

without food or water. He would return to camp for just ten days and then go away to fast again. The third brother put up sweat lodges and invited certain men to participate in sweat baths every day. Whenever the band moved camp, he would build sweat lodges and ask the men to join him again. The fourth brother gave feasts to his clan fathers, whenever he had deer or buffalo meat. He feasted his clan fathers nearly every day. The brothers worshiped in these four different ways to see who would prosper in the world.

They began in the spring and continued through the summer and into the fall. When

The People and Culture of the Crow

Every year, the Crow celebrate their traditions with a powwow.

the leaves were falling from the trees, the Sweater told the people to have their children bring beads for an offering and gather sticks for the sweat lodge fire. He promised them that their children would grow up and have children of their own. There was no sickness and many people had many children because the Sweater had done what was right. He lived to be one hundred years old before he died.

The Sun Worshiper gave anything he got to the Sun. After a while, he made a willow hoop to which he tied four sharp, black sticks and a handle with buffalo-hair rope. He tied a feather to each of the four points and attached sagebrush between the sticks. To the handle, he tied a square piece of blanket painted with a black circle. As soon as the Sun rose, he raised the sacred hoop to the light and prayed, and the Sun warned him of the approach of their enemy. After many sacrifices and struggles, the Crow prevailed, and the Sun Worshiper lived to be ninety years old.

The Feaster went hunting every day to feed his clan fathers. Since he feasted his clan fathers and offered gifts to them so often, he seldom went on the warpath. Even when he went on a raid, he promised to give a horse to one of his clan fathers if he counted coup. He lived to be one hundred years old. He was so old that when the band moved camp, his skin tore.

The fourth brother, who was the Faster, hardly stayed at home. He remained home for only a day or two before going away again. He would dig a hole and lie down through the days and nights without food or water. He often cried, but one night he also heard some enemy warriors who were planning to raid the camp of his people. He returned to camp and remained there, so that he could help defend the band. He killed a warrior and then moved camp with his band. He lived to be forty years old and brought good fortune to his people.

These four brothers all became prominent men. The Feaster and the Sweater became the oldest, followed by the Sun Worshiper and the Faster. All did well and brought much good to their people.

Today, storytelling is still very much a part of Crow life. Ancient stories and practices have been passed down over the generations. While many Native people have turned toward Christianity as their main religion, the original Crow traditions are still performed with respect and dedication. These traditions will no doubt continue as more generations of Crow people come to learn about and appreciate their heritage.

A Crow warrior, Holds the Enemy, wears more Western-style clothing.

CHAPTER FIVE

Education is your most powerful weapon.

—Chief Plenty Coups

OVERCOMING HARDSHIPS

When Europeans and Americans first settled in Crow territory, the tribes were initially peaceful and friendly towards the newcomers. They had heeded the advice of Old Man Coyote and treated the white men with respect, lest they risk offending the god and endangering their culture. However, as settlers claimed more and more Native land, conflicts eventually threatened the relationship between the groups. The Crow were faced with a new era of fear, sadness, and war.

The Crow people's lives changed forever with the arrival of settlers and the advent of railroads.

Conflict Begins

The Crow and the new settlers originally lived side by side without much tension. The two groups of people at first helped each other and traded with each other for furs, food, and other precious goods. However, in the mid-nineteenth century, all of that began to change.

Settlers traveling westward into Crow territory began to want more land to build towns and cities and to pave the way for railroads. The Crow viewed land as a gift and not something that could be owned. However, settlers had different views and wanted to claim the land on which the Crow lived for themselves. The Crow took this issue up with the government. In 1851, the Crow took part in the First Treaty of Fort Laramie. In this **treaty**, Crow territory was formally recognized as a vast sweep of prairie in Montana and Wyoming, encompassing 38.5 million acres (15.6 million hectares), mostly in the Yellowstone region. This protected the land of the Crow and other Native tribes. After the Civil War, however, the United States government demanded that the Crow surrender most of this land. In 1868, by terms of the Second Treaty of Fort Laramie, they lost over three-fourths of this land to the federal government, leaving about 9 million acres (3.6 million ha) for a reservation south of the Yellowstone River. During this time, the Crow became less nomadic, as they settled in winter camps where many people moved into log cabins.

War and Oppression

During the 1860s and 1870s, the Crow warriors—including the famous Chief Plenty Coups—were allied with US Army soldiers in several battles against their traditional enemies among the Plains tribes. Serving as scouts, they fought with American troops primarily against the Nez Percé, Sioux, and Cheyenne. Several warriors were scouts for Lieutenant Colonel George Armstrong Custer and the Seventh Cavalry before the American defeat at the Battle of Little Bighorn in 1876. Despite all their support for the United States, however, the Crow were not treated any better by the federal

This illustration shows the Montana Crow Indian Reservation, circa 1887.

government than the Plains tribes that had fought against American forces. However, US Army soldiers did later protect the Crow from deadly attacks by the Sioux.

By the early 1880s, waves of miners, trappers, and settlers had moved into Crow territory, building forts and laying tracks for railroads. By 1883, as the buffalo vanished from the Great Plains, the Crow faced starvation, and their traditional life quickly ended. The Crow came to depend on people called Indian **agents** for the basic necessities of food, clothing, and shelter. They were forced to move onto a reservation established at Crow Agency, Montana, in 1883.

Many settlers thought the only way to accept the Native people was to "civilize" the entire Native population. They took many steps to do so, including

The People and Culture of the Crow

building special schools that taught them American traditions, encouraging them to dress in the American style, and restricting or even forbidding their Native customs. For example, new laws passed in 1883 forbade ceremonies including the Sun Dance and the popular Plains gift-giving ceremonies called giveaways. Daily activities were restricted as well. For instance, it became illegal to leave the reservation without permission from the agent or to sell a horse to another Native person. People had to apply for a pass from the Indian agent if they wanted to hunt off the reservation. Special reservation police, who reported only to the agent, arrested people for breaking any rule and hauled them before the Court of Indian Offenses. After a brief trial, offenders were punished with fines, reduction of rations, or forced labor. Already impoverished, people could scarcely afford these added hardships for such minor offenses.

People tried to concentrate on new social groups like the Hot Dance and Crazy Dog societies, both of which had been acquired from the Hidatsa around 1875. They also liked to reminisce about war exploits and trade with the Sioux, Cheyenne, and other tribes.

In the early years on the reservation, young men occasionally slipped away on horse raids or to pursue Blackfeet raiders. During this time, the Blackfeet and Crow were swept up in minor conflicts, trying to raid and take each others' horses. This escalated in 1887, when a warrior named Wraps Up His Tail returned from a raiding party. He and his comrades had successfully taken horses back from the Blackfeet and went to the Indian agent to celebrate. Their setting off of rifles alarmed the agent, who called for

Chief Arapoosh's shield, thought to possess prophetic powers, circa 1830

backup from nearby Fort Custer. US Cavalry and the Crow police, overseen by Chief Plenty Coups, tried to restrain Wraps Up His Tail, but he and his men fled to the mountains. Eventually, the conflict ended when Wraps Up His Tail was shot dead.

Unlike other Native nations, the Crow did not take part in the **Ghost Dance** religion, which swept across the plains. This religion taught that the earth would cover up all the settlers and the buffalo would return to the Great Plains. For the most part, the Crow respected and worked alongside settlers. This changed somewhat as the nation lost more and more of the land it once called home. Most notably, in 1825 Chief Arapoosh refused to sign a treaty of peace with the US government, one that was signed by leaders of other Crow bands. This led to some bitterness.

During the late 1880s, the Crow had to cede more of their remaining lands. By 1886, 250 people were living on their own parcels of land. However, the Dawes Act of 1887 provided for further **allotment**. This act changed the way many Native nations' lands were structured. Rather than having land belong to the tribe, the Dawes Act stated that the president had the authority to divide land and assign it to an individual Native person. This also scattered land holdings of family members, which weakened the Crow community. Much of the land allotted was on dry desert, unsuitable for substantial farming, which led to problems. Facing unfavorable conditions, many Crow families were not interested in farming, so they sold their allotted land to non-Natives until Crow territory became a checkerboard of plots owned by Natives and settlers. For those who did choose to farm, the small 160-acre (65 ha) allotments could support only a few head of cattle, which was not enough to support a family. Inheritance further divided these small holdings. In 1890 and 1905, the US government made further purchases of Crow land. In the 1890 agreement, the Crow lands were reduced to about 3 million acres (1.2 million ha). By 1905, the reservation had dwindled to 2.3 million acres (930,000 ha), which was just a fraction of the territory once roamed by the

Crow. The tribe continued to lose more land through the early years of the twentieth century. Today, it stands at 2 million acres (80,900 ha).

Over the years, Crow beliefs and customs were further threatened as schools were established on or near the reservation. Starting in 1883, some Crow children were sent to Carlisle Indian Industrial School in Pennsylvania. This school sought to assimilate Native children into American lifestyles, habits, and beliefs. Essentially, the school wanted the Native children to abandon all Native practices, languages, and traditions. Between 1886 and 1907, the Roman Catholic Church founded mission schools at Saint Xavier, Pryor, Lodge Grass, Crow Agency, and Wyola. In 1904, the Baptist Home Mission School opened in Lodge Grass, Montana. By 1905, government boarding schools at Crow Agency had around 225 students.

Over the course of the nineteenth century, the Crow population dwindled. In 1806, when Lewis and Clark ventured into Montana, there were about 3,500 Crow, living in about 350 lodges. By 1834, the population had grown to about 4,500 people. However, smallpox and other European diseases for which Native people had little resistance struck Crow bands. In 1890, their population had fallen to 2,287. By the 1890s, the remaining Crow had abandoned traditional methods of providing food, clothing, and shelter. They faced starvation and overwhelming poverty. By 1904, their numbers plunged to 1,826. Through the twentieth and twenty-first centuries, however, the population steadily recovered. As of 2015, 7,900 people lived on the reservation and tribal enrollment stood at 13,000.

The People and Culture of the Crow

Dancers at the Crow Fair powwow

A Language Preserved

The Crow speak a Siouan language. Many other Plains tribes, including the Mandan, Sioux, Assinoboine, and Omaha, also spoke Siouan languages. However, Crow is more closely related to Hidatsa—since the Crow and Hidatsa were a single tribe until only a few hundred years ago. The Crow language is still widely spoken today by most children and adults on the reservation. The language is now taught in reservation schools.

The following examples are based on *A Dictionary of Everyday Crow* compiled by Mary Helen Medicine Horse and *Crow Language Learning Guide* compiled by Edith C. Kates and Hu Matthews for the Bilingual Materials Development Center, Crow Agency, Montana. Crow can be a challenging language, but the alphabet and pronunciation key should help in understanding a few words.

The Crow alphabet has twenty-six letters, but not c, f, g, j, r, v, y, and z. The alphabet includes twelve vowels: *a, e, i, o, u, aa, ee, ii, oo, uu, ia, ua*. The first five single letters are short vowels, the five double letters (digraphs) are long vowels. The last two (*ia* and *ua*) are **diphthongs**. The vowels are pronounced as follows:

a	as in h*u*t
aa	as in f*a*ther
e	as in b*e*t
ee	as in *a*ble
i	as in b*i*t
ii	as in b*ea*t
o	as in g*o*t
oo	as in b*o*de
u	as in p*u*t
uu	as in b*oo*t
ia	as in *area*
ua	as in Nash*ua*

There are fifteen consonants: *b, ch, d, h, k, l, m, n, p, s, sh, t, w, x,* and *?*. The letter *?* is the glottal stop, or a catch in the throat, as in the space between "uh-oh!" Five of the consonants (*l, m, n, w,* and *?*) never appear at the beginning of a Crow word.

The consonants are generally pronounced as in English. However, when the letter *p* appears between vowels or follows *h* or *x*, it sounds like the English language *b*. The double *kk* has a stronger *k* sound, but between vowels, it is similar to the *g* in "game." The letter *t* has the same sound as in English, but when between vowels or preceded by *h* or *x*, it sounds more like the English *d* in "day." The digraph *ch* sounds like the *ch* in "chicken," except between vowels or after *h* and *x* when it sounds similar to the *j* in "jump." The digraph *sh* is similar to the *sh* in "sheep," except between vowels when it is similar to the *s* in "pleasure."

Each of the double letters, or digraphs, and diphthongs (*ia* and *ua*) represents a single sound. The stress mark indicates the part of the word that is spoken loudest. In diphthongs, it also indicates pitch. If the accent is on the first letter, the sound goes slightly up, then down. If on the second letter, the pitch rises slightly.

The following are some everyday words used by the Crow.

People

ichuuké	brother (younger)
aksaawacheé	father
isbaapíte	grandchild
chilée	husband
bacheé	man
isahké	mother
isahkáate	sister (older)
uá	wife
bíakalishte	woman (young)

Animals

áapxaxxe; úuxkaashe	antelope
dúuptakoishe	bald eagle
daxpitchée	bear

bilápe	beaver
dakáake	bird
búattee	coyote
úuxe	deer
bishkakaáshe; bishké	dog
iichíilikaashe	elk
buá	fish
iichíile	horse
iishbíia	mountain lion
baapúxte	otter
chihpé	prairie dog
iisashpíte	rabbit
xuáhchee	skunk
ishtaléeschia	squirrel
cheéte	wolf

Natural World

dappuulé	blizzard
xakúpw	canyon
amnía	cliff
ahpaaxé	cloud
chilía	cold
shichúushe	foothills
baákahpee	hail
shiché	hill
kalíhchiia	lightning

dachkalanneé	mist
bilítaachiia	moon
awaxaawé	mountain
alawachúhke	plains
xaleé	rain
awáxe	sky
bíia; bíihpe	snow
ihké	star
áxxaashe	sun
suuá	thunder
huché	wind

Seasons

basée	autumn
áwasiia; bíawakussee	spring
bíawakshe	summer
báalee	winter

Although life for the Crow has not been easy, their perseverance has proven them capable of overcoming obstacles and embracing their traditions. Their communities may have changed since they first arrived in North America, but their history and heritage live on in the hearts and souls of the first Crow people's descendants. Today, the tribe has much to celebrate and of which to be proud.

The reservation at Crow Agency continues today.

CHAPTER SIX

Respect yourself ... learn your native language ... and listen to your parents and elders.

—Darrin Old Coyote, 21st Chairman of the Crow Nation

THE NATION'S PRESENCE NOW

The Crow Nation has evolved into a thriving community that continues to celebrate its ancestry, heritage, and traditions. As caretakers of 2 million acres (800,900 ha) of land, the Crow communities living in the Northwest have remained closely tied to their heritage. Today, many Crow people continue to raise horses and participate in yearly communal events, such as the Sun Dance, the celebration of which was reinstated by the Crow Nation in 1941. The Crow still face hardship, but the nation as a whole is improving and evolving with the ever-changing twenty-first century.

A Crow Revival

The Crow began to revive their culture in 1934 when the tribe refused to adopt some provisions of the Indian Reorganization Act. This act reversed some of the conditions of the Dawes Act, namely the allocation of land from the tribe to an individual. Future allotment of land went to the tribe rather than individuals, and any surplus land was also returned to the care of the tribe. The act likewise allowed for nations to have more independence and self-governance. One of the first steps in this was to draft tribal constitutions. The Crow did jus that. Under the leadership of Chief Robert Yellowtail, they adopted their own constitution in 1948. Since that time, the Crow have been governed by a general council made up of all adult enrolled members of the tribe. Any person age eighteen or older may take part in council meetings—which are similar to town meetings—by voicing opinions and voting on issues. The government itself consists of four elected officials, including a chairperson, vice-chairperson, secretary, and vice-secretary, all of whom are elected every four years. There are also several tribal committees, which oversee the administration of a number of tribal programs.

Like other tribes, the Crow have been involved in disputes regarding land claims and land rights over the years. In the 1950s, the tribe was forced to sell its land rights in Bighorn Canyon to the US government,

Robert Yellowtail was an important part of twentieth century Crow history.

which planned to build a dam there. It received $9.2 million from the US government in 1961, and another $2 million in 1963 for the dam property. When completed, the project was ironically named Yellowtail Dam and Reservoir, after Robert Yellowtail. However, this thoughtful tribal leader had adamantly opposed the project. The funds received for these lands were applied to other land purchases and an industrial development program on the reservation.

Today, the reservation's lands are tribally owned, allotted to individuals, or owned by non-Natives. Although the Crow have lost most of their territory over the years, they still have the largest reservation in Montana. Crow Agency is located in Big Horn and Yellowstone Counties, Montana, southeast of Billings, along Interstate 90. Its southern border is Wyoming.

This map shows where the Crow Reservation is located.

The tribe also retains mineral rights to 1.1 million acres (445,000 ha) near Billings and Hardin, Montana, and near Sheridan, Wyoming.

The Nation Today

Through the twentieth and twenty-first centuries, the Crow have struggled economically. It has been difficult to attract industry to the relatively isolated region of the reservation. Some tribal lands have been placed in agricultural production—fields for crops and pastures for grazing cattle. Like other reservations on the northern plains, most of the rangelands on the reservation are now leased to non-Native ranchers who graze large herds of beef cattle. The tribe also manages leases for gas, oil, and coal. It also receives some income from timber, fisheries, and hunting rights. This income is desperately needed, but the leases and rights do not provide many jobs. A casino and tourism activities provide some jobs on the reservation. However, there are many people who need work. According to a *Los Angeles Times* article from December 2014, unemployment stands at 47 percent.

Finding enough work for people has always been challenging, but it is especially difficult for the Crow and other Native people living on reservations. The Crow largely depend on money generated from coal production to sustain themselves. When in 2014 President Barack Obama and the Environmental Protection Agency suggested reducing carbon emissions from power plants by 30 percent, the Crow chairman Darrin Old Coyote said such a move would "be devastating to us." The Crow control mineral rights to an estimated 9 billion tons (8.2 million metric tons) of coal. Losing revenue from coal production would leave a significant hole in the Crow Nation's annual budget.

What other resources they do have are in the form of education and cultural preservation. Since the time of Plenty Coups, the Crow have continued to emphasize education and the preservation of traditional culture, including their language. In 1918, they started an annual powwow known as Crow Fair, one of the oldest powwows and largest Native American gatherings in North America. Held every August, Crow Fair becomes the "Tepee Capital of the World," with cone-shaped tipis dotting the landscape. Over the course of several days, Crow Fair includes rodeos, parades, and powwows. The Crow display their elaborately beaded floral patterns on clothing and horse gear in

A young woman performs the Fancy Social Dance at the Crow Fair.

The People and Culture of the Crow

Little Big Horn College educates many young men and women.

the parades. In 2015, this festival celebrated its ninety-seventh anniversary, and it continues to enjoy a good turnout of local and international attendees.

In 1941, religious leader William Big Day revived the Sun Dance, which is now held on sacred grounds on the reservation. This dance has sacred and ancestral significance and continues to be performed despite previous attempts to stop it. In 1980, the Crow established Little Big Horn College, a two-year community college on the reservation. The college offers several associate's degrees and certificates that specifically aim to benefit the Crow Nation as well as community employers. Originally only having thirty-two students enrolled, today the college reports having at least three hundred students enrolled every term.

In 2003, new buildings were dedicated and officially opened. There are also modern elementary and high schools on the reservation. High school teams have won several state titles in basketball, and individuals have been recognized for their achievements in track.

Tourism

One of the other main draws of the Crow Nation area is tourism. The Crow are remembered for their bravery in the face of seemingly impossible situations. Throughout their history, they have been involved in many confrontations. That history, coupled with Montana's rich landscape, attracts many people year-round to the area. One of the most popular tourist attractions on the Crow reservation is the site of the Little Bighorn Battlefield National Monument, which honors the soldiers and warriors who were killed in the historic fight. Every summer, the Crow hold a reenactment of the battle along Little Bighorn Creek. Likewise, the US Cavalry School offers eight-day classes on riding, while also educating participants in dress, Native culture, and weapon handling like the 1870s US Cavalry.

Billings, Montana, and the Crow Nation lands have also been the settings of many movies and television series, such as *Little Big Man* (1970), *Nebraska* (2013), *The Amazing Race* (2001), *Undercover Boss* (2010), and *Hotel Impossible* (2012). Film companies choose Montana for its powerful scenery, historical significance, and its open spaces.

The Crow people hope to develop an economy that thrives and preserves the traditions first passed down from their earliest ancestors. Without heritage, history,

The People and Culture of the Crow

Dustin Hoffman in *Little Big Man*, some of which was filmed at Crow Agency.

and resources, the Crow's present lifestyle would cease to exist. Today the Crow is a proud nation that has endured much and persisted through great adversity. They are strong in spirit and determined to make their lives and their lands better for future generations to enjoy and discover.

Crow chief Darrin Old Coyote (*left*) and secretary Alvin Not Afraid (*right*) sign an agreement in January 2013 to expand coal mining on their lands.

CHAPTER SEVEN

*I would have you
cling to the memories
of your fathers.*

—Chief Plenty Coups

FACES OF THE CROW NATION

Throughout history, there have been many notable people belonging to Crow tribes. These men and women have earned a place in the nation's rich history. For their efforts and their accomplishments, they are remembered here.

Arapoosh (Arapooish, Eripuass, Rotten Belly) (circa 1790–1834), war chief, lived along the Bighorn, Powder, and Wind Rivers in what are now northern Wyoming and southern Montana. As he grew up, he became a renowned warrior in conflicts against the Blackfeet, Northern Cheyenne, Sioux, and other traditional enemies of the Crow. Before a raid or battle, Arapoosh's shield was rolled. If it fell face up, the Crow went ahead with the attack. If it fell face down, the campaign was abandoned. Suspicious of officials of the US government, Arapoosh refused to sign a Crow treaty of friendship with the United States in 1825. He died soon afterward in a battle with the Blackfeet.

Blackfoot (ca. 1795–1877), principal chief, lived with his Mountain Crow band north of the Yellowstone River and south of the Musselshell River in present-day Montana. In the 1850s, he became a chief and in the 1860s, he was chosen as head chief of his band. As leader of his people, he took part in many councils with US government officials. These included meetings at Fort Laramie, Wyoming, in 1868, and at Crow Agency, Montana, in 1873. At the Crow Agency council, he made several speeches to members of the Board of Indian Commissioners in which he protested the settling of Crow lands. He died of pneumonia near the present-day town of Meeteetse, Wyoming.

Curly (Curley, Ashishishe, Shishi'est, the Crow) (ca. 1859–1923), scout and research informant, was born along the Rosebud River in what is now Montana. As a young man, he allied with American settlers and soldiers,

Chief Blackfoot

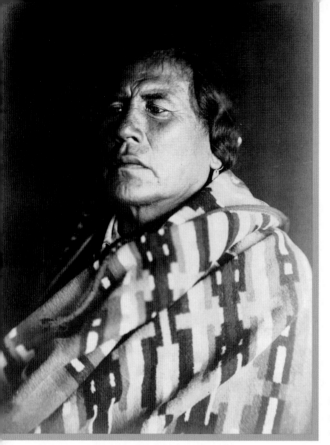

Curly was the sole survivor of the Custer massacre.

as encouraged by Chief Plenty Coups. With his brother White Swan, Curly served as a scout under a Crow leader named White-Man-Runs-Him with Lieutenant Colonel George Armstrong Custer's Seventh Cavalry. He claimed that he was wounded at the Battle of Little Bighorn in 1876. He said that he escaped by hiding his Crow clothing under the blanket of a dead Sioux warrior and slipping away. However, White-Man-Runs-Him and other scouts reported that they had been sent to the rear before the fighting started, which enabled them to escape. At the fork of the Bighorn and Yellowstone Rivers, Curly encountered an army supply boat and reported Custer's defeat. He later provided information to scholars who were researching the famous battle.

The People and Culture of the Crow

Plenty Coups (Aleek-chea-ahoosh, Many Accomplishments) (ca. 1848–1932), head chief, was born near the present-day city of Billings, Montana. His father, Medicine Bird, was Crow and Shoshone, while his mother was a full-blooded Crow. When he was about fourteen, Plenty Coups climbed into the Crazy Mountains on a vision quest. There he dreamed of a chickadee, which tribal leaders later interpreted to mean that he should seek to live peacefully with the settlers moving into Crow territory. Although he became a great warrior in raids and battles against traditional Native enemies, he never fought against American soldiers.

During the Black Hills War of 1876–1877, Plenty Coups helped to provide scouts for General George Crook in his campaign against Sioux warriors led by Sitting Bull and Crazy Horse. Crow scouts, such as Curly and White-Man-Runs-Him, served with Lieutenant Colonel George Armstrong Custer at Little Bighorn. The Crow also served as scouts in the campaign against the Nez Percé led by Chief Joseph. Because of his knowledge of the English language, Plenty Coups represented the Crow in negotiations with the Northern Pacific Railroad. He also traveled to Washington, DC, to lobby for Crow land claims.

In 1904, Plenty Coups succeeded Pretty Eagle as principal chief of the Mountain Crow. During World War I, he encouraged tribal members to enlist in the armed forces. After the war, in 1921, he was asked to represent all Native Americans at the Tomb of the Unknown Soldier at Arlington, Virginia. To close the ceremony, the old chief reverently placed his warbonnet and coup stick on the grave. At age eighty,

Chief Plenty Coups (*center*) and two warriors attend a dedication.

Plenty Coups donated his home and 40 acres (16.18 ha) to be made into a public park for people of all races. The site is now a state park with a museum about Crow history and customs. After Plenty Coups's death at Pryor, Montana, in 1932, the Crow honored him by eliminating the title "tribal chief," which made him the last of the Mountain Crow chiefs.

Pretty Shield (1856–1944), healer, was a well-respected woman and member of the Crow tribe Sore Lips. She was named after her grandfather's war shield and remained with the Crow tribe her entire life. She became a healer after experiencing a vision

The People and Culture of the Crow

in which a woman guided her to an anthill and told her to ask for anything she wanted. She requested a good life, and ever after that the "ant people" were her medicine guides. Pretty Shield married a warrior named Go Ahead at the age of sixteen. Following the death of her husband, she raised her five surviving children and nine grandchildren mostly on her own. Pretty Shield was commemorated and celebrated by famed biographer Frank Linderman in his 1932 book *Pretty-shield: Medicine Woman of the Crows*. The book was republished in 2003 with a new forward, allowing further generations to understand and celebrate this remarkable woman's life and accomplishments.

Two Leggings

Two Leggings (His Eyes Are Dreamy) (ca. 1845–1923), warrior and research informant, was born along the Montana River. He grew up to become a warrior of the River Crow. He made raids against the Sioux and other traditional enemies of the Crow, but never against American settlers or migrants passing through the territory of his people. Between 1919 and 1923, he shared the story of his life with William Wildschut, a businessman and amateur anthropologist, working under sponsorship of the Museum of the American Indian and the Heye Foundation. Peter Nabokov edited these research notes into a book entitled *Two Leggings: The Making of a Crow Warrior*, which was published in 1967. Two Leggings died at his home near Hardin, Montana. He was survived by his wife, Ties-Up-Her-Bundle, and two adopted children.

White-Man-Runs-Him

White-Man-Runs-Him (Miastashedekaroos, Mahrstahsheedahkuroosh, Mars-che-coodo) (ca. 1855–1925), scout, research informant, was the son of a Crow warrior of the same name who had been mocked and forced to run past a white man with a gun. Yet, as was the case with many other Crow warriors who had long been enemies of the Sioux, he served with the US army as a scout, as suggested by Plenty Coups. As head scout for Lieutenant Colonel George Armstrong Custer's Seventh Cavalry, he was present at the Battle of Little Bighorn in June 1876. After finding the large Sioux encampment, he reported to Custer and was

The People and Culture of the Crow

sent to the rear, which enabled him to escape from the defeat. Along with Curly, he later gave information about the battle to researchers.

These men and women led inspiring and spirited lives. Today, their courage and abilities are remembered and celebrated. They are symbols of Crow perseverance and pride. Without them, or the people before them, the history of the Crow people would have unfolded in a very different way.

CHRONOLOGY

1600s Around sixty million buffalo roam the Great Plains.

ca. 1730 The Crow acquire horses and learn to become expert riders. Nomadic buffalo hunters, they become one of the dominant tribes of the Great Plains.

1803 The United States purchases the Louisiana Territory from France, a vast area that included Crow territory and led to westward expansion. In the following years, trading posts are established throughout the West.

1806 Lewis and Clark expedition encounters Crow during exploration of the Louisiana Territory.

ca. 1825 The Crow split into two main groups that become known as the Mountain Crow and River Crow.

1837–1870 At least four smallpox epidemics ravage the tribes of the Great Plains.

1849 The United States government purchases Fort Laramie from the American Fur Company and posts troops there.

1851 The Crow are one of the eleven tribes to sign the First Treaty of Fort Laramie, in which their territory is defined as 38.5 million acres (15.6 million ha) in Montana and Wyoming.

1862 The Homestead Act leads to a flood of settlers on Native lands, including the Great Plains. The Crow decide not to fight settlers or migrants through their territory.

1868 The Second Treaty of Fort Laramie takes away three-quarters of the land from the 1851 treaty and grants a reservation for the Crow south of the Yellowstone River in Montana.

1876 The Crow provide scouts for Lieutenant Colonel George Armstrong Custer and his forces at the Battle of Little Bighorn.

1883 Crow forced to move onto reservation at Crow Agency, Montana. The US government prohibits the Sun Dance of the Plains People.

1887 The General Allotment Act, or Dawes Act, reduces Native land by giving 160 acres (64.7 ha) to each family and 80 acres (32.3 ha) to individuals, with "surplus lands" opened for settlement.

1900 Fewer than one thousand buffalo remain on the Great Plains.

1924 The United States recognizes all Native Americans born within the states and territories as citizens.

1934 The Indian Reorganization Act recognizes tribal governments and provides financial assistance, but the Crow refuse to adopt provisions of this act.

1941 The Sun Dance is revived on the Crow Reservation—and has been performed nearly every summer since.

1948 The Crow adopt their own constitution and establish a tribal government.

1980 Little Big Horn College is established on the reservation in Crow Agency.

2003 The Crow complete major new buildings at Little Big Horn College.

2015 The Crow host the 97th Annual Crow Fair in Crow Agency, Montana.

GLOSSARY

Absaroka Crow name for themselves, which means "Children of the Long-Beaked Bird."

agent A United States government employee responsible for undertaking official business with a Native tribe.

Akíssatre A society that served as camp police to maintain peace and order.

allotment A United States government policy of dividing tribal lands in the 1800s into small tracts owned by individuals. Also, one of the tracts.

band Small group of related family members who lived and traveled together.

Bering Strait The body of water that separates Russia and Alaska. During the last Ice Age, a land bridge across the strait allowed for migration from one continent to the other.

berm A small wall of dirt or sand.

breechcloth A cloth or skin worn between the legs; also breechclout.

buckskin Animal hide softened by a tanning or curing process.

buffalo chips Dried buffalo droppings, which the Crow and other Plains People used for fuel.

clan Members of a group who consider themselves related through a common ancestor.

counting coup Touching an enemy in battle to prove one's bravery.

cradleboard A wooden board used to carry a baby.

diphthong Two vowel sounds in one syllable; together they form a speech sound; e.g., *oy* of "boy" or *ou* of "out."

fur trade Network in which the Crow traded animal furs, especially beaver pelts, for metal tools, guns, and other goods that rapidly changed their way of life.

Ghost Dance Religious movement that swept the Great Plains in the 1800s in which people believed that settlers would vanish and the traditional ways would return if people danced and performed certain rituals.

giveaway Popular ceremony of the Crow and many Plains tribes, in which families offer gifts to honor a relative, to express appreciation, or to accept a new responsibility.

Great Plains Vast area of prairie stretching across the North American heartland, extending north to south from Canada to Texas.

moccasins Soft leather shoes often decorated with brightly colored beads.

mustang Wild horse of the western plains and Rocky Mountain region.

nomadic Moving frequently from one place to another.

Old Man Coyote According to Crow mythology, the supreme being who created the world.

parfleches Rawhide pouches for storing food and belongings.

pemmican Pounded dry meat mixed with fat and berries, often eaten during the winter or when the Crow traveled.

phratry Group made up of two or three clans that shared in various activities.

quillwork Decorative embroidery patterns created with the quills of porcupines or birds.

rock medicine Stone kept in a pouch or worn on a necklace for good luck or protection.

shaman Holy person who is responsible for the spiritual and physical healing of tribal members. Also medicine man.

sweat lodge Dome-shaped hut covered with buffalo skins in which purification and other sacred ceremonies are held.

tipi Cone-shaped home made of poles covered with animal skins.

travois Sled made of two poles lashed together and pulled by a dog or horse.

treaty Signed, legal agreement between two nations.

warbonnets Feathered headdresses worn by Crow warriors.

BIBLIOGRAPHY

Bauerle, Phenocia. *The Way of the Warrior: Stories of the Crow People*. Lincoln, NE: Bison Books, 2004.

Crow, Joseph Medicine. *Counting Coup: Becoming a Crow Chief on the Reservation and Beyond*. Washington, DC: National Geographic Children's Books, 2006.

——. *From the Heart of the Crow Country: The Crow Indians' Own Stories*. Lincoln, NE: Bison Books, 2000.

Donlan, Leni. *Counting Coup: Customs of the Crow Nation*. American History Through Primary Sources. Chicago, IL: Raintree, 2006.

Dunbar-Oritz, Rozanne. *An Indigenous Peoples' History of the United States*. ReVisioning American History. Boston, MA: Beacon Press, 2014.

Hill, Rick, and Terri Frazier. *Indian Nations of North America*. Washington, DC: National Geographic, 2010.

Linderman, Frank B. *Plenty-Coups: Chief of the Crows*. Lincoln, NE: Bison Books, 2002.

——. *Pretty-shield: Medicine Woman of the Crows*. 2nd ed. Lincoln, NE: Bison Books, 2003.

Loeb, Barbara, and Mardell Hogan Plainfeather. *Lillian Bullshows Hogan, the Woman Who Loved Mankind: The Life of a Twentieth-Century Crow Elder*. Lincoln, NE: Bison Books, 2012.

Lowie, Robert H. *The Crow Indians*. 2nd ed. Lincoln, NE: Bison Books, 2004.

MacDonald, Douglas H. *Montana Before History: 11,000 Years of Hunter-Gatherers in the Rockies and Plains*. Missoula, MT: Mountain Press Publishing Company, 2012.

Parrett, Aaron. *Montana: Then and Now*. Bozeman, MT: Bangtail Press, 2014.

Rzcezkowski, Frank. *Uniting the Tribes: The Rise and Fall of Pan-Indian Community on the Crow Reservation*. Lawrence, KS: University Press of Kansas, 2012.

Snell, Alma Hogan. *A Taste of Heritage: Crow Indian Recipes and Herbal Medicines*. At Table. Lincoln, NE: Bison Books, 2006.

Strandberg, Greg. *A History of Montana: Braves and Businessmen*. Volume III. Montana History Series. Seattle, WA: Amazon, 2014.

Walter, Dave. *Montana Campfire Tales: Fourteen Historical Narratives*. 2nd ed. Guilford, CT: TwoDot Press, 2011.

FURTHER INFORMATION

Want to know more about the Crow Nation? Check out these websites, videos, and organizations.

Websites

Crow Nation

tribalnations.mt.gov/crow

This website offers statistics and historical information about the Crow Nation.

Cultural Heritage of the Crow

serc.carleton.edu/research_education/nativelands/crow/culture.html

This webpage provides detailed information about the Crow's cultural heritage and where the Crow are today.

National Geographic: The Crow

www.nationalgeographic.com/lewisandclark/record_tribes_002_19_21.html

This website gives a brief history of the Crow Nation.

Videos

**Crash Course US History: The Black Legend,
Native Americans, and Spaniards**

www.youtube.com/watch?v=6E9WU9TGrec

This video briefly explains circumstances and situations facing Native American tribes after the Europeans arrived.

**We Are Still Here: A Documentary on Today's
Young Native Americans**

www.youtube.com/watch?v=HnPKzZzSClM

Young Native Americans today explain what it was like growing up with their culture and heritage.

Organizations

Crow Nation Executive Branch

PO Box 129

Crow Agency, MT 59022

(406) 638-3708

www.crow-nsn.gov

Little Big Horn College

8645 South Weaver Drive

Crow Agency, MT 59022

(406) 638-3100

www.lbhc.edu

The Montana Historical Society
225 N. Roberts Street
PO Box 201201
Helena, MT 59620-1201
(406) 444-2694
mhs.mt.gov

INDEX

Page numbers in **boldface** are illustrations. Entries in **boldface** are glossary terms.

The People and Culture of the Crow

other uses of, 52, 56,
60–61, 70
vanishing of, 58, 80, 83
buffalo chips, 52
Bull Owners society, 31

Carlisle Indian Industrial
School, 84
casino, 95
ceremonies, 25, 28, 56,
65–67, 69, 81, 105
story of, 70–71, 74–75
See also Bear Song;
Cooked Meat
Singing; giveaway;
Sun Dance
Cheyenne, 18–19, 27, 48, 79,
81, 102
chiefs, 11, 30–32, 48–49, 56,
106
children, **6**, 26–28, 36, **40**,
41–43, **42**, 45–46, 84–85,
96
Christianity, 75, 84
Civil War, 79
clan, 27–30, 32, 36, 41, 65,
71–72
clothing, 12, 14, 17, 23, 26,
28, **44**, 47, 52–52, 58–59,
59, 60, **75**, 80, 84, 95

See also breechcloth;
moccasins
coal, 94–95, **101**
constitution, 92
Cooked Meat Singing, 65–67
cooking, 27, 35–36, 40–41,
51–52, 60
recipe, 50
counting coup, 18–19, 32,
48–49, 54, 74
Court of Indian Offenses,
81
cradleboard, 26, 40–41,
40, 61
crafts, 59–61
See also parfleches;
quillwork
Crazy Horse, 105
creation myth, 14–17
Crook, George, 105
Crow Agency, 80, 84–85,
90, 93, 95, **99**, 102
Crow Fair, **85**, 95, **96**, 97
Curly, 102, 104–105, **104**,
109
Custer, George
Armstrong, 79,
104–105, 108

tools, 26, 34, 60–61

tourism, 95, 98

trading, 12, 17–18, **19**, 25, 51, 53, 58, 78, 81

travois, **11**, 12, 26, 33, 41, 51

treaty, 79, 83, 102

Two Leggings, 107–108, **107**

United States military, 79–81, 98, 103–105, 108

vision quest, 45, 65, **69**, 105

warbonnets, 17, 54, 105

warfare, 18–19, 21, 25–27, 29–32, **31**, 36, 39, 41–43, 45–46, **46**, 48–49, 53–54, 58, 60–61, 64, 66, **66**, 79–81, 98, 102, 104–108 *See also* Battle of Little Bighorn; Black Hills War; Civil War; World War I

war societies, 30–31, 48, 81

Washington, DC, 105

weapons, 18–19, **18**, 32, 36, 41, 48, 59–61

weather, 13, 23, 53

White-Man-Runs-Him, 104–105, 108–109, **108**

White Swan, 104

Wildschut, William, 107–108

World War I, 105

Wraps Up His Tail, 81

Wyoming, 10, 79, 93–94, 102

Yellowstone River, 11, 13–14, 64, 79, 102, 104

Yellowtail, Robert, 92–93, **93**

ABOUT THE AUTHOR

Raymond Bial has published more than eighty books—most of them photography books—during his career. His photo-essays for children include *Corn Belt Harvest, Amish Home, Frontier Home, Shaker Home, The Underground Railroad, Portrait of a Farm Family, With Needle and Thread: A Book About Quilts, Mist Over the Mountains: Appalachia and Its People, Cajun Home,* and *Where Lincoln Walked.*

As with his other work, Bial's deep feeling for his subjects is evident in both the text and illustrations. He travels to tribal cultural centers, photographing homes, artifacts, and surroundings and learning firsthand about the national lifeways of these peoples.

The emeritus director of a small college library in the Midwest, he lives with his wife and three children in Urbana, Illinois.